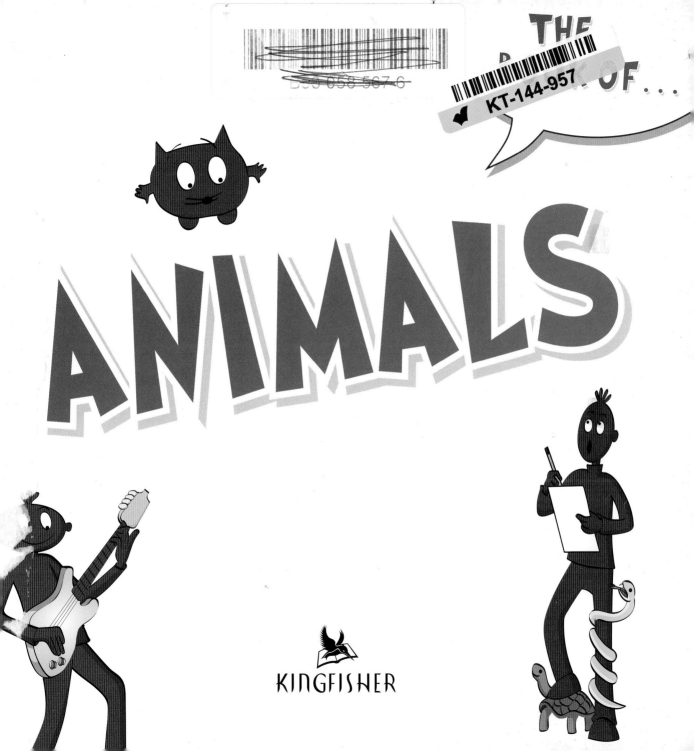

THE
BOOK OF...

ANIMALS

KINGFISHER

KINGFISHER

First published 2013 by Kingfisher
an imprint of Macmillan Children's Books
a division of Macmillan Publishers Limited
20 New Wharf Road, London N1 9RR
Basingstoke and Oxford
Associated companies throughout the world
www.panmacmillan.com

Written and Illustrated by Dynamo Limited
Concept by Jo Connor

ISBN 978-0-7534-3643-1

Copyright © Macmillan Children's Books 2013

10 9 8 7 6 5 4 3 2 1
1TR/0413/LFG/UG/140MA

A CIP catalogue record for this book is
available from the British Library.

Printed in China

WHAT'S IN THIS BOOK?

ANIMALS

HAVE YOU EVER WONDERED WHY... OR WHAT... OR WHEN?

It's only natural to wonder about the world around us. It's a very complicated and surprising place sometimes. And you'll never understand what is going on around you unless you ask yourself a question every now and again.

We have investigated the natural world to collect as many tricky questions as we could find about animals...

...and we also found the answers for you!

We now invite you to come with us on an exploration of the animal kingdom, so that we can show you all the answers we have discovered.

4

We also thought it might be fun to see how much of this shiny new knowledge you can remember – so at the back of the book, on pages 56 and 57, you'll find some Quick-Quiz questions to test you out. It's not as scary as it sounds – we promise it will be fun. (And besides, we've given you all the answers on pages 58 and 59.)

While we were searching for all those answers, we found out some other pretty interesting things, too. We wrote them all down on these panels – so you can memorize these facts and impress your friends!

QUICK-QUIZ QUESTIONS

Did you know...

There are about one million species of insects we know about, but scientists think there are millions more waiting to be discovered.

Are you ready for this big adventure?

Then let's go!

HOW MANY ANIMALS ARE THERE IN THE WORLD?

Nobody knows how many animals there are in the world, or even how many species (types of animal) exist. Scientists have discovered and named around 1.5 million species so far. About three-quarters of them are insects.

Did you know...

Beetles are the biggest group of insects found so far. More than 375,000 different types of beetle have been discovered.

WHY ARE PLANTS NOT ANIMALS?

Most animals can move from one spot to another, but plants cannot. They do not eat food like animals do, either. They make their own food using sunlight, and they soak up water through their roots. A plant's cells – the tiny building blocks of its body – are made differently to an animal's cells, too.

HOW DO ANIMALS GET THEIR NAMES?

Animal names come from lots of different languages. For example, 'giraffe' comes from 'zirafa' - a very old, Arabic word meaning 'long neck'. Each animal has a scientific Latin name, too, normally chosen by the person who discovered it.

GIRAFFE

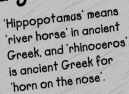

Did you know...

'Hippopotamus' means 'river horse' in ancient Greek, and 'rhinoceros' is ancient Greek for 'horn on the nose'.

HAVE WE DISCOVERED EVERY ANIMAL THERE IS?

It is thought there are millions of animal species still to be discovered. Some scientists think there might be more than nine million species altogether on Earth, but there is no way of knowing for sure. Around 15,000 new species are found each year.

Did you know...

Scientists believe that most of the Earth's big animals have now been found - small animals make up most of the new discoveries.

WHAT'S SPECIAL ABOUT INSECTS?

An insect has six legs and three parts to its body – a head at the front, a thorax in the middle and an abdomen at the back. It has no backbone, but it does have an exoskeleton – hard body parts like armour on the outside of its soft body.

Did you know...

We know from studying fossils that insects existed on Earth 390 million years ago. The earliest ones were cockroaches and dragonflies.

DO INSECTS LIVE EVERYWHERE?

Insects live everywhere on Earth except under the ocean. They can live in freezing-cold or baking-hot places and on high mountains - locations where other animals find it very hard to survive.

11

WHY DO SOME INSECTS BUZZ?

The buzzing of a fly or a bee is the sound of its wings beating very fast as it flies through the air. Flies are among the fastest of all flying insects – their wings beat about 200 times a second. The bigger a bee is, the slower its wings beat, and the lower its buzz sounds.

Did you know...

Some types of bee vibrate their body and wings extra fast when they visit flowers, to knock pollen off. When they do this, they buzz very loudly for a moment.

HOW BIG DO INSECTS GROW?

The largest bee in the world can grow up to 4.5 centimetres long. It buzzes around the Indonesian island of Bacan, but luckily its sting is weaker than the sting of a normal-sized honeybee.

The longest insect in the world is the Indonesian giant stick insect, which can grow up to 35 centimetres long. The heaviest insect is the African Goliath beetle, which weighs up to 100 grams, roughly the weight of an apple.

WHICH INSECT MAKES NOISES WITH ITS LEGS?

A male grasshopper has tiny pegs on its back legs. It rubs the pegs against its wings to make a noise that attracts female grasshoppers. Some other male insects, such as crickets, rub their wings together to make a sound.

Did you know...

A tiny water boatman insect called *Micronecta scholtzi* makes the loudest noise of any creature in the world for its size. People walking beside European rivers can sometimes hear its buzzing sound floating up from the surface of the water.

WHICH INSECT HAS A STINKY SHOOTING WEAPON?

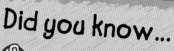

Did you know...

? The blister beetle oozes a nasty chemical that is capable of making human skin burn and blister.

The Devil's coach horse beetle shoots a jet of stinking liquid from its stomach to frighten off attackers. The bombardier beetle has a similar weapon, shooting out boiling-hot chemicals that it cooks up inside its body.

15

HOW BIG CAN A SWARM OF INSECTS GET?

In 1875, more than 12 trillion locusts swarmed across western USA, covering over 513,000 square kilometres! It was the biggest swarm ever recorded – bigger than the entire US state of California. It was bad news for local farmers, because locusts eat crops.

Did you know...

A locust eats its own weight in plants every day, so a million locusts will eat around a tonne of food a day. Usually, locust swarms contain billions of locusts.

WHICH CREEPY-CRAWLY HAS THE MOST LEGS?

Millipedes have the most legs in the animal world. They are related to insects, but instead of having six legs, they have up to 750. The biggest ones live in Africa and grow to about 24 centimetres long.

WHY ISN'T A SPIDER LIKE A FLY?

A
ZKLM
T BDOP

Did you know...

Most spiders have bad eyesight. They rely on their senses of touch and taste to find their way around.

Spiders are arachnids, not insects. They have eight legs, not six, and two body parts instead of three. They do not have antennae (feelers) like insects do, and they never have wings. Most spiders have eight eyes, whereas most insects have two.

HOW BIG CAN A SPIDER GROW?

The world's biggest spider is the South American Goliath bird-eating spider. It can grow to up to 30 centimetres wide and weigh more than 120 grams. It lives in a burrow in the ground and hunts small snakes, lizards and frogs, but very rarely birds.

Did you know...

The Goliath bird-eating spider is a type of tarantula. When they are threatened, tarantulas shoot out their sharp body hairs like tiny spears.

HOW DO FISH SWIM SO SPEEDILY?

Did you know...

There are around 22,000 known fish species. They range in size from the tiny, 7.9-millimetre-long *Paedocypris* fish to the giant, 14-metre-long whale shark.

Fish have bodies that are thin and streamlined, which means they can cut through water quickly. They swim by flicking their tail from side to side, using their fins to steer.

WHICH FISH WOULD WIN IN A FISH RACE?

Did you know...

Fish have a swim bladder – a small, gas-filled balloon shape inside their body that helps to keep them afloat underwater.

The Indo-Pacific sailfish holds the record for swimming the fastest. Its speed has been measured at 112 kilometres per hour, although it can travel this fast only in short bursts.

WHICH SHARK HAS THE BIGGEST MOUTH?

The biggest fish in the sea is the whale shark. Its giant mouth is 1.4 metres wide, but this monster is quite gentle. To feed, it swims with its mouth wide open, filtering (sieving) tiny creatures from the seawater.

Did you know...

The biggest ever shark, the megalodon, lived about 20 million years ago. It may have grown up to 17 metres long, and it had fearsome, 15-centimetre-long teeth!

WHICH SHARK LOOKS LIKE A CARPET?

Carpet sharks have beautiful patterns on their skin. They live on the bottom of shallow seabeds. The biggest one, the spotted wobbegong, grows to about three metres long and has shaggy fringes on its body to camouflage (hide) it amongst the seaweed.

Did you know...

There are lots of different types of shark, including the goblin shark, the prickly shark, the cow shark, the angel shark, the zebra shark and the lemon shark.

23

WHICH UNDERSEA ANIMAL CAN OPEN A JAR?

Octopuses are amongst the cleverest creatures in the sea. In aquariums, some octopuses have worked out how to unscrew jar lids, just by watching how it is done by humans. They are thought to have a good memory, too.

Did you know...

Some octopuses can detach and drop one of their arms if they are attacked. While their attacker is distracted by the crawling arm, the octopus can get away. Later, it can regrow the lost arm.

WHAT IS THE MOST POISONOUS ANIMAL IN THE WORLD?

The box jellyfish is the world's most poisonous creature. It drifts in the waters of the Pacific Ocean, trailing its tentacles, which can grow up to three metres long. Each tentacle is covered in deadly stinging cells.

Did you know...

Some fish, such as the lionfish and the surgeonfish, have poisonous spikes on their body to protect themselves from attack.

DEADLY POISONOUS

WHICH FISH CAN FLY?

Did you know...

Flying fish can glide along for up to 100 metres. They do this to escape their undersea enemies.

When a flying fish launches itself above the ocean it looks as if it's flying, but really it is gliding using its wing-like fins. It dips its tail into the water to push itself along.

WHICH FISH CAN CLIMB TREES?

Did you know...

Climbing gourami fish can use their bony fins to walk on land. These fish are found in African and Indian rivers.

The mangrove killifish lives in the mangrove swamps of Latin America, on the edge of the ocean. When the swamps dry up, it changes its gills so that it can breathe air. It then climbs a tree, and can hide there for up to two months before the swamp water returns.

WHAT CROAKS, HOPS AND SWIMS UNDERWATER?

Did you know...

When they are underwater, frogs breathe through their skin.

Frogs can hop around on land or swim underwater. They are in a group of animals called amphibians, which includes toads and newts, too. Frogs are famous for their fantastic jumping skills and can leap up to 20 times their own length.

DO FROGS LIVE IN TREES?

Some frogs spend all of their lives in trees, laying their eggs in pools of rainwater that collect on tree leaves. Tree frogs are good at climbing because they have tiny, sticky pads on their feet.

Did you know...

The South American poison dart frog has deadly poisonous slime on its skin. It is the most poisonous land animal in the world.

HOW IS A HUMAN LIKE A BLUE WHALE?

Humans and blue whales both belong to a family of animals called mammals. All mammals are vertebrates, which means they have a backbone. Mammal mothers feed their babies with milk, which most other animal families don't do. There are more than 5,000 species of mammal.

Did you know...

New mammals are very rarely discovered, but in 2008 a new species, the giant elephant shrew, was found in Tanzania. It is the size of a cat and has a nose that looks like a small trunk.

WHO HAS THE BIGGEST BABIES IN THE WORLD?

The blue whale is the largest animal that has ever lived, and has the biggest babies of any creature. Newborn baby blue whales measure around seven metres long and can weigh as much as a small truck! They are born tail-first underwater.

Did you know...

Baby giraffes are around 1.8 metres tall when they are born - roughly as tall as an adult male human.

DO ELEPHANTS GET ANGRY?

Did you know...

When elephants get excited they run around in circles, trumpeting and rumbling. They often do this when they meet old friends.

Elephants are among the most intelligent mammals, and they display lots of different feelings. They get angry if they are threatened, and have the power to crush and kill another creature, even one as big as a rhino.

WHAT DO LIONS DO MOST?

Lions sleep for between 14 and 16 hours a day because they need a lot of energy for hunting, which quickly tires them out. They usually sleep during the day and hunt at night.

WHICH BIG MAMMAL HAS TINY BABIES?

Kangaroos grow up to two metres tall but newborn kangaroo babies are only around two centimetres long (about the size of a peanut in its shell). The tiny baby, called a joey, has stumps instead of legs. It stays inside its mother's pouch and feeds on milk while it grows.

Did you know...

The smallest mammal in the world is the bumblebee bat, found in Borneo. An adult measures between 30 and 40 millimetres long.

WHICH **MAMMAL** HAS **POISONOUS SPIKES?**

The male duck-billed platypus has a poisonous spike (called a spur) on each of its back legs. Its venom is strong enough to kill an animal the size of a dog. The duck-billed platypus lives in eastern Australia.

WHICH IS THE LOUDEST MAMMAL?

The blue whale is the loudest animal on Earth. Its song, a low whistle, is louder than the noise made by a jet plane! The sound travels through water to reach other whales. The loudest land animal is the South American howler monkey, whose impressive whooping can be heard nearly five kilometres away.

Did you know...

Whales learn new songs when they travel to a new area. They copy the songs of the whales they meet.

WHICH MAMMAL IS THE SMELLIEST?

Some mammals, such as skunks and polecats, defend themselves by spraying stinky fluid from scent glands in their bottom. The African striped polecat's spray is the smelliest. It can be detected up to 800 metres away – the length of eight football pitches.

WHAT DOES A DOG'S BARK MEAN?

Dogs have lots of different types of bark, which they use to communicate with other animals. They bark to show happiness, unhappiness, fear, to send out a warning and to make friends.

Did you know...

A dog that is very upset might howl, and dogs will make a whining noise if they want something, such as food or exercise.

WHEN DO MICE SING LIKE BIRDS?

Did you know...

Male and female gibbons sing duets with each other that can last for up to 30 minutes.

When male mice want to attract female mice, they sing like birds. They make very tiny tweeting noises that are too high-pitched for humans to hear.

CAN ALL BIRDS FLY?

Although all birds have feathers and wings, they do not all have the ability to fly. Penguins use their wings to swim, for instance. Ostriches and emus, the biggest birds in the world, cannot fly but they can run very fast.

Did you know...

An ostrich can run at speeds of up to 64 kilometres per hour, to get away from danger.

WHICH BIRD LAYS THE BIGGEST EGGS?

Today, it is the North African ostrich that lays the world's biggest egg. It is the size of a large melon, and weighs about the same as 24 chicken's eggs.

Did you know...

The New Zealand elephant bird is now extinct (no living examples are alive today), but it once laid the biggest eggs of any bird ever. Each of its eggs measured about 90 centimetres around the middle.

WHEN IS A BIRD LIKE A BEE?

The world's tiniest bird, the bee hummingbird, is only about 5.7 centimetres long. It lives in Cuba, where it lays the world's smallest bird eggs – they are only around six millimetres long. This bird builds itself a tiny, thimble-sized nest out of moss and cobwebs.

WHICH BIRD CAN SWIM SUPER-FAST UNDERWATER?

The gentoo penguin can swim at up to 40 kilometres per hour in the ocean. It lives on islands in the Antarctic. On land it waddles around clumsily, but in the water it can twist and turn acrobatically.

Did you know...

Penguins can dive well, too. Emperor penguins can dive to 450 metres below the surface and stay underwater for up to 18 minutes.

WHICH BIRDS ARE THE BEST BUILDERS?

Birds build all kinds of different nests. The biggest nests are giant mounds of earth, leaves and sticks made by the dusky scrubfowl of Indonesia. Scrubfowl mounds can measure up to 12 metres across and tower five metres high.

Did you know...

Swallows and martins build their nests from pellets of mud mixed with their spit.

DO BIRDS DECORATE THEIR HOMES?

Did you know...

Some male bowerbirds paint their dens with yellow or purple plant juice to make them more bright and colourful.

Some birds are very house-proud. The male bowerbird of Australia tries to attract a female by building a den of sticks decorated with treasures he has collected, including flowers, beetle wings, pretty feathers, snail shells and man-made things such as keys or scraps of fabric.

WHY DO SNAKES LIKE TO SUNBATHE?

Snakes are reptiles, a family of cold-blooded animals. They cannot heat their bodies through chemical reactions, as we do, so they bask in sunlight to warm up and keep their body functions working at normal speed. This also gives them the energy to hunt for food.

Did you know...

During the warmer times of the year, snakes will come out at night to hunt. When it is cold, they hide somewhere safe and rest.

COULD A SNAKE SWALLOW A HUMAN?

Did you know...

? The fossil of the titanoboa, the largest snake ever found, was discovered in a South American coal mine. It measured 13 metres in length!

Snakes can open their jaws much wider than we can. They can grab an animal bigger than their own head and swallow it whole. Very big snakes could probably swallow a small human.

WHICH LIZARD CAN WALK ON WATER?

South American brown basilisk lizards are so small and light that they can skitter across water quickly without sinking. They live on riverbanks and in rainforests, and use their clever water-walking trick to escape from enemies.

Did you know...

The tiny pygmy gecko is only two to four centimetres long. It is so light that it can float on the surface of water. Its waterproof skin acts like a tiny wetsuit.

WHICH LIZARD HAS SUPER-STICKY TOES?

Did you know...

Scientists have studied gecko toe hairs to recreate this special ability and make super-strong, sticky gecko 'tape'.

Geckos are a type of lizard that can walk upside down on ceilings. They have millions of very tiny hairs on the pads of their toes, which act like strong glue and keep them from falling.

WHY IS A LIZARD'S TONGUE A SECRET WEAPON?

Some lizards have a 'ballistic' tongue that they can fire out at top speed to grab a tasty insect. The chameleon has a super-fast tongue like this, which is sometimes longer than the rest of its body. Its tongue is covered in thick, gooey spit, which sticks to its prey.

HOW DO YOU KNOW WHEN A CHAMELEON IS ANGRY?

Did you know...

The African Namaqua chameleon uses its colour to stay cool or warm. It goes dark in the cool morning to absorb heat, but turns lighter to reflect heat as the day grows warmer in its desert home.

Chameleons can change the colour of their scaly skin to indicate their mood or to camouflage (hide) themselves. A chameleon will go darker when it is angry or wants to scare an enemy. It will turn lighter and more patterned to impress a mate.

CAN CROCODILES TALK?

Did you know...

Baby crocodiles chirp from inside their eggs when they are about to hatch, to signal to their mum that they are ready to come out.

Crocodiles are very chatty reptiles. They cough, grunt, hiss, roar and rumble to communicate with each other. Each crocodile has its own distinctive-sounding voice.

HOW CAN YOU TELL AN ALLIGATOR FROM A CROCODILE?

Did you know...

Crocodiles and alligators can run quite fast over short distances on land.

Alligators and crocodiles are both reptiles, but they look different. Alligators have a wide snout, which is good for crushing animals such as turtles. Crocodiles have a narrower snout, which is better for catching fish. An alligator's lower teeth are hidden when its mouth is shut.

WHAT KIND OF ANIMAL IS AN EARTHWORM?

An earthworm is from a family of animals called annelids. They have no bones or limbs, but they do have tiny hair bristles on their body to help them to slide along.

WHY ARE EARTHWORMS SO SLIMY?

Earthworms do not have lungs. They breathe through their skin, but they can do this only if their skin stays wet, so they make body slime to keep themselves moist.

Did you know...

 Earthworms that get chopped in half do not survive as two separate worms, but an earthworm can regrow the tip of its tail if it gets cut off.

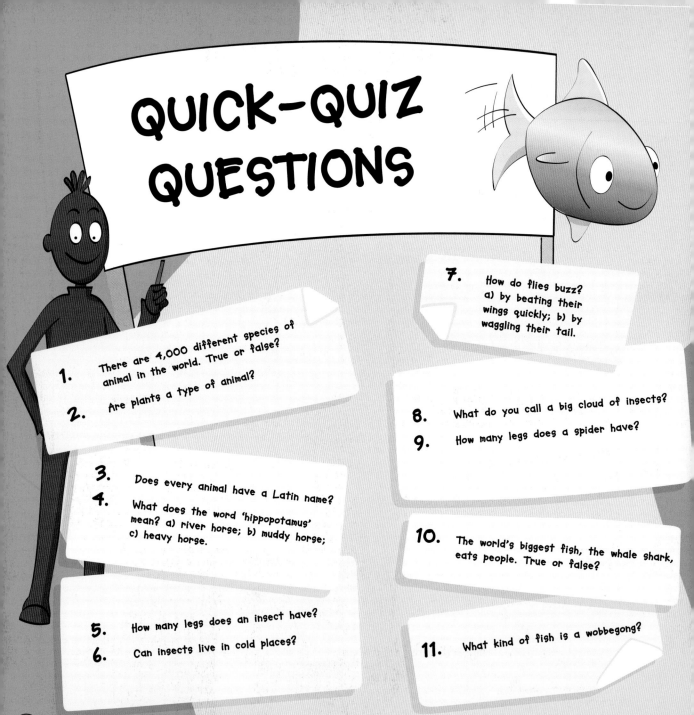

QUICK-QUIZ QUESTIONS

1. There are 4,000 different species of animal in the world. True or false?

2. Are plants a type of animal?

3. Does every animal have a Latin name?

4. What does the word 'hippopotamus' mean? a) river horse; b) muddy horse; c) heavy horse.

5. How many legs does an insect have?

6. Can insects live in cold places?

7. How do flies buzz? a) by beating their wings quickly; b) by waggling their tail.

8. What do you call a big cloud of insects?

9. How many legs does a spider have?

10. The world's biggest fish, the whale shark, eats people. True or false?

11. What kind of fish is a wobbegong?

12. Where does a box jellyfish have its sting? a) on top of its head; b) on its tentacles; c) inside its mouth.

13. Do flying fish fly by flapping their wings, like birds?

14. Can some fish climb trees?

15. Is a frog a reptile or an amphibian?

16. Do all mammals have a backbone?

17. How long does a lion sleep for each day? a) 2-3 hours; b) 7-9 hours; c) 14-16 hours.

18. What is a baby kangaroo called?

19. In which country does the duck-billed platypus live?

20. Which living bird lays the world's biggest eggs?

21. Can penguins fly?

22. What type of animal is a snake?

23. What type of reptile is a gecko? a) a lizard; b) a snake.

24. Do lizards have eyelids or not?

25. When an alligator has its mouth closed, can you see its bottom teeth or not?

QUICK-QUIZ ANSWERS

1. False. There are around 1.5 million known animal species.
2. No.
3. Yes. Each animal has a Latin name, which is its scientific name.
4. a) river horse.
5. Six legs.
6. Yes. Insects live everywhere except under the ocean.
7. a) by beating their wings quickly.
8. A swarm.
9. Eight legs.
10. False.
11. A shark.

12. b) on its tentacles.

13. No. They glide using wing-like fins.

14. Yes.

15. An amphibian.
16. Yes. All mammals have a backbone.

17. c) 14–16 hours.

18. A joey.

19. Australia.
20. An ostrich.

21. No.
22. A reptile.

23. a) a lizard.

24. Lizards have no eyelids.
25. You cannot see its bottom teeth.

TRICKY WORDS

AMPHIBIAN
A family of animals that can live both in water and on land.

ANNELID
A family of animals with no bones or limbs. Earthworms are annelids.

ANTENNAE
Sensitive feelers that some animals use to help them sense the world around them.

ARACHNID
A family of animals that have eight legs and no backbone. Spiders are arachnids.

BACKBONE
A series of small bones form the spine (backbone) of some animals. Humans have a backbone.

BALLISTIC
If something is ballistic, it is able to move extremely quickly and with force. Some lizards have a 'ballistic' tongue, which they can flick out very fast.

CAMOUFLAGE
The colours or patterns on an animal's skin or fur that help it to blend in with its surroundings.

CELLS
The tiny building blocks that make up the bodies of living things.

CHAMELEON
A type of lizard that can change the colour of its skin.

COLD-BLOODED
When an animal's temperature is controlled by its surrounding environment, rather than by its own body's chemical reactions.

ELECTROPERCEPTION
The ability to detect the electrical signals given out by animals when they move their muscles.

EXOSKELETON
A hard covering, like armour, on the outside of an animal's body. Insects have exoskeletons.

FILTER
To sieve out tiny pieces from a liquid. Some whales feed by filtering out tiny creatures from seawater.

FIN
A flat body part that helps creatures such as fish to balance, move or steer in the water.

FOSSIL
The ancient, preserved remains of an animal or a plant found in rock.

GILL
Gills are the special body parts that allow fish to extract oxygen from water, which they need for breathing.

GLAND
A body part that makes chemicals for the body to use. A skunk makes a stinky liquid in its scent glands to scare off other animals.

INSECT
A family of animals that have six legs, three main body sections and no backbone.

LATIN
The language spoken in ancient Rome, used today for the scientific names of animals.

MAMMAL
A family of animals that feed their young with the mother's milk, and have a backbone. Humans are mammals.

MANGROVE
A type of tree that can grow in salty water, on the edge of a sea.

POLLEN
A fine powder produced by flowers, containing the material needed to make new plant seeds.

REPTILE
A family of cold-blooded animals with scaly skin. Most reptiles lay soft-shelled eggs.

SPECIES
A particular type of animal.

STREAMLINED
A smooth shape.

SWIM BLADDER
A small, gas-filled pouch – a bit like a balloon – inside a fish's body, which helps the fish to float at different depths underwater.

TENTACLE
A long, thin feeler that some creatures have. Tentacles grow out from an animal's head.

THORAX
The middle section of an insect's three-part body.

VENOM
A type of poison made by an animal.

VERTEBRATE
An animal with a spine, or backbone ('backbone' is also in this glossary).

VIBRATE
To shake very quickly.

WHERE TO FIND STUFF

Wow! What an amazing
journey! We hope you had
as much fun as we did, and learnt
many new things. Who knew there was
so much to discover about animals!
Here are some other exciting books
where you'll find more to explore:

The Book Of... How?
The Book Of... What?
The Book Of... Where?
The Book Of... Which?
The Book Of... Who?
The Book Of... Why?
The Book Of... Dinosaurs
The Book Of... The Human Body
The Book Of... Space

Look out for these great books!
'Who' knows 'what' we'll
discover... See you soon!

Zany Tongue-Twisters

Joseph
Rosenbloom
& Mike Artell

Illustrated by
Steve Harpster

S   N York

Library of Congress Cataloging-in-Publication Data Available

10   9   8   7   6   5   4   3   2   1

Published in paperback in 2005 by Sterling Publishing Co., Inc.
387 Park Avenue South, New York, NY 10016
© 2003 by Sterling Publishing Co., Inc.
Much material excerpted from *The Little Giant Book of Tongue Twisters*
© 1999 by Mike Artell, and some twisters excerpted from *World's Toughest*
Tongue Twisters © 1986 by Joseph Rosenbloom.
Distributed in Canada by Sterling Publishing
℅ Canadian Manda Group, 165 Dufferin Street,
Toronto, Ontario, Canada M6K 3H6
Distributed in Great Britain and Europe by Chris Lloyd at Orca Book
Services, Stanley House, Fleets Lane, Poole BH15 3AJ, England
Distributed in Australia by Capricorn Link (Australia) Pty. Ltd.
P.O. Box 704, Windsor, NSW 2756, Australia

Printed in China

Sterling ISBN 1-4027-0865-3 Hardcover
        ISBN 1-4027-2774-7 Paperback

For information about custom editions, special sales, premium and
corporate purchases, please contact Sterling Special Sales
Department at 800-805-5489 or specialsales@sterlingpub.com.

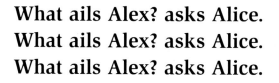

Arnie's oranges aren't as orange
as Arnold's oranges.

What ails Alex? asks Alice.
What ails Alex? asks Alice.
What ails Alex? asks Alice.

*How many times can you say
this in ten seconds?*
Alice asks for axes.

Apes ate Kate's cake.
Apes ate Kate's cake.
Apes ate Kate's cake.

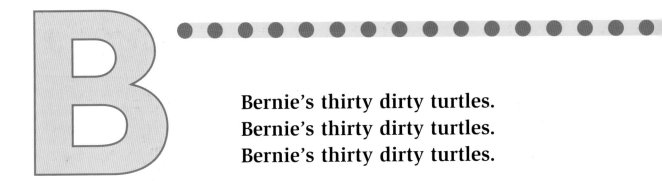

B

Bernie's thirty dirty turtles.
Bernie's thirty dirty turtles.
Bernie's thirty dirty turtles.

A big bug hit a bold bald bear.
A big bug hit a bold bald bear.
A big bug hit a bold bald bear.

Brandy bandaged the bear.
Brandy bandaged the bear.
Brandy bandaged the bear.

Bad black bran bread.
Bad black bran bread.
Bad black bran bread.

A box of mixed biscuits
  and a biscuit mixer.

Brenda Black was blameless.
Brenda Black was blameless.
Brenda Black was blameless.

How many times can you say this in ten seconds?

Big blue bubbles.

Bess's pet pestered Fess.
Bess's pet pestered Fess.
Bess's pet pestered Fess.

Byron's butler brought Byron's brother butter.
Byron's butler brought Byron's brother butter.
Byron's butler brought Byron's brother butter.

Bring the black boot back.
Bring the black boot back.
Bring the black boot back.

The fuzzy bee buzzed the buzzy busy beehive.
The fuzzy bee buzzed the buzzy busy beehive.
The fuzzy bee buzzed the buzzy busy beehive.

Three blind mice blew bugles.
Three blind mice blew bugles.
Three blind mice blew bugles.

How many times can you say this in ten seconds?
Bob's blue blobs.

A cheeky chimp.
A cheeky chimp.
A cheeky chimp.

A canner exceedingly canny
One morning remarked to his granny,
"A canner can can
Anything that he can,
But a canner can't can a can, can he?"

How many times can you say this in ten seconds?
Chop suey shop.

Does this shop stock cheap checkers?
Does this shop stock cheap checkers?
Does this shop stock cheap checkers?

A cupcake cook in a cupcake cook's cap.
A cupcake cook in a cupcake cook's cap.
A cupcake cook in a cupcake cook's cap.

Chester chucked chestnuts.
Chester chucked chestnuts.
Chester chucked chestnuts.

"Cheep, cheep," chirped the cheery chick.
"Cheep, cheep," chirped the cheery chick.
"Cheep, cheep," chirped the cheery chick.

Who checked the chart of the cud-chewing cow?
Who checked the chart of the cud-chewing cow?
Who checked the chart of the cud-chewing cow?

Charles chose the chief cheap sheep section.
Charles chose the chief cheap sheep section.
Charles chose the chief cheap sheep section.

How many times can you say this in ten seconds?

The drummers drummed and the strummers strummed.

Does a double bubble gum double bubble?
Does a double bubble gum double bubble?
Does a double bubble gum double bubble?

Dave's dogs dig deep ditches.
Dave's dogs dig deep ditches.
Dave's dogs dig deep ditches.

11

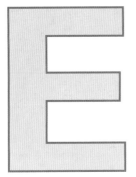

E

Eddie's enemies envied Eddie's energy.
Eddie's enemies envied Eddie's energy.
Eddie's enemies envied Eddie's energy.

**Every errand Randy ran
for Erin was in error.**

Eleven little leather loafers.
Eleven little leather loafers.
Eleven little leather loafers.

How many times can you say this in ten seconds?
Eight eager elephants.

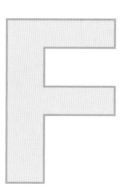

Can a flying fish flee far from a free fish fry?
Can a flying fish flee far from a free fish fry?
Can a flying fish flee far from a free fish fry?

For fine fresh fish, phone Phil.
For fine fresh fish, phone Phil.
For fine fresh fish, phone Phil.

A fish sauce shop's
  sure to sell fresh
  fish sauce.
A fish sauce shop's
  sure to sell fresh
  fish sauce.
A fish sauce shop's
  sure to sell fresh
  fish sauce.

Friendly fleas and fireflies.
Friendly fleas and fireflies.
Friendly fleas and fireflies.

Friendly fleas and huffy fruit flies.
Friendly fleas and huffy fruit flies.
Friendly fleas and huffy fruit flies.

How many times can you say this in ten seconds?
French shrimp shop.

Fifty-five flags flutter freely.
Fifty-five flags flutter freely.
Fifty-five flags flutter freely.

A fat-free fruit float.
A fat-free fruit float.
A fat-free fruit float.

How many times can you
say this in ten seconds?
   Free flag.

The fly fled fat Flo's flat.
The fly fled fat Flo's flat.
The fly fled fat Flo's flat.

Frank Fry's father.
Frank Fry's father.
Frank Fry's father.

Three fluffy feathers.
Three fluffy feathers.
Three fluffy feathers.

How many times can you say this in ten seconds?

Grape cakes.

Gus goes by Blue Goose bus.
Gus goes by Blue Goose bus.
Gus goes by Blue Goose bus.

The cruel ghoul cooks gruel.
The cruel ghoul cooks gruel.
The cruel ghoul cooks gruel.

How many times can you
say this in ten seconds?
Gabby gray gobblers.

Great gray geese graze.
Great gray geese graze.
Great gray geese graze.

The grave groom grew glum.
The grave groom grew glum.
The grave groom grew glum.

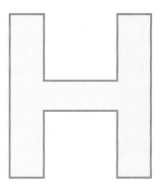

Hillary's hairy hound hardly hurries.
Hillary's hairy hound hardly hurries.
Hillary's hairy hound hardly hurries.

How many times can you say this in ten seconds?

Heed the head henpecker!

The hairy hare stares
  at the hairier hare.
The hairy hare stares
  at the hairier hare.
The hairy hare stares
  at the hairier hare.

Imagine managing an imaginary menagerie.
Imagine managing an imaginary menagerie.
Imagine managing an imaginary menagerie.

I'll lie idle on the isle.
I'll lie idle on the isle.
I'll lie idle on the isle.

How many time can you say this in ten seconds?

Six sick insects.

Jill's giraffe juggled
jam jars.
Jill's giraffe juggled
jam jars.
Jill's giraffe juggled
jam jars.

*How many times can you say
this in ten seconds.*
Just dust.

Jack's giraffe juggled jelly jars.
Jack's giraffe juggled jelly jars.
Jack's giraffe juggled jelly jars.

K

Keep clean socks in a clean sock stack.
Keep clean socks in a clean sock stack.
Keep clean socks in a clean sock stack.

Knee deep, deep knee.
Knee deep, deep knee.
Knee deep, deep knee.

How many times can you say this in ten seconds?
A knapsack strap.

King Kong plays Ping Pong.
King Kong plays Ping Pong.
King Kong plays Ping Pong.

A lump of red leather, a red leather lump.
A lump of red leather, a red leather lump.
A lump of red leather, a red leather lump.

Ladylike lowland llamas.
Ladylike lowland llamas.
Ladylike lowland llamas.

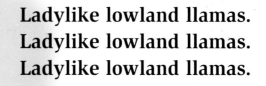

Larry's lair lacks locks.
Larry's lair lacks locks.
Larry's lair lacks locks.

How many times can you say this in ten seconds?
Lemon-lime liniment.

Lee loves to rob lobsters.
Lee loves to rob lobsters.
Lee loves to rob lobsters.

Local loggers' lawyers.
Local loggers' lawyers.
Local loggers' lawyers.

He who laughs last laughs late.
He who laughs last laughs late.
He who laughs last laughs late.

Little licorice lollipops.
Little licorice lollipops.
Little licorice lollipops.

Luminous aluminum.
Luminous aluminum.
Luminous aluminum.

How many times can you say this in ten seconds?
Long lush lashes.

M

I miss my Swiss Miss and my Swiss Miss misses me.
I miss my Swiss Miss and my Swiss Miss misses me.
I miss my Swiss Miss and my Swiss Miss misses me.

Monster mother's muffins.
Monster mother's muffins.
Monster mother's muffins.

Much mushroom mash.
Much mushroom mash.
Much mushroom mash.

How many times can you say this in ten seconds?
Matt's mismatched mittens.

How many times can you say this in ten seconds?

Nine nimble noblemen.

Ninety-nine knitted knickknacks
 were nicked by ninety-nine knitted knickknack nickers.

I need not your needles,
They're needless to me,
For the needing of needles
Is needless, you see.
But did my neat trousers
But need to be kneed,
I then should have need
Of your needles indeed.

Ollie oils oily autos.
Ollie oils oily autos.
Ollie oils oily autos.

How many times can you say this in ten seconds?
One worm wiggled.

Orville ordered ordinary ornaments.
Orville ordered ordinary ornaments.
Orville ordered ordinary ornaments.

Pass the pink peas please.

Please prune plum trees promptly.
Please prune plum trees promptly.
Please prune plum trees promptly.

The parrot pecked the pirate's pet.
The parrot pecked the pirate's pet.
The parrot pecked the pirate's pet.

Polly placed a plate of pasta
on Peter's pizza parlor poster.

A peck of pesky pixies.
A peck of pesky pixies.
A peck of pesky pixies.

Pat pet Peg's pig.
Pat pet Peg's pig.
Pat pet Peg's pig.

*How many times can you
say this in ten seconds?*

**Polly planted potted
plants.**

**Poor pure Pierre.
Poor pure Pierre.
Poor pure Pierre.**

**People pay pros for playing.
People pay pros for playing.
People pay pros for playing.**

**Pretty precious plants.
Pretty precious plants.
Pretty precious plants.**

Pretty promising peace prospects.
Pretty promising peace prospects.
Pretty promising peace prospects.

How many times can you say this in ten seconds?
Is a pleasant peasant's pheasant present?

Pale pink plumage.
Pale pink plumage.
Pale pink plumage.

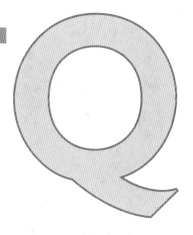

The quack quit asking questions.
The quack quit asking questions.
The quack quit asking questions.

The queen coined quick quips.
The queen coined quick quips.
The queen coined quick quips.

Quakes cause cracks.
Quakes cause cracks.
Quakes cause cracks.

Russ was the wristwatch rust remover.
Russ was the wristwatch rust remover.
Russ was the wristwatch rust remover.

Rex wrecks wet rocks.
Rex wrecks wet rocks.
Rex wrecks wet rocks.

Wanda raised white roses.
Wanda raised white roses.
Wanda raised white roses.

How many times can you say this in ten seconds?

Rush the washing, Russell.

Real rear wheels.
Real rear wheels.
Real rear wheels.

Round and round the rugged rocks the ragged rascal ran.

The right fruit is ripe fruit.
The right fruit is ripe fruit.
The right fruit is ripe fruit.

S

No shipshape ship's shop
stocks shop-soiled shirts.

*How many times can you say
this in ten seconds?*
Slick silk socks.

Seth's sharp spacesuit shrank.
Seth's sharp spacesuit shrank.
Seth's sharp spacesuit shrank.

The spunky skunk and the stinky slug.
The spunky skunk and the stinky slug.
The spunky skunk and the stinky slug.

Sixteen sloppy, smelly slippers.
Sixteen sloppy, smelly slippers.
Sixteen sloppy, smelly slippers.

*How many times can you say this
in ten seconds?*
Six crisp snacks.

Is Sherry's shortcake shop shut?
Is Sherry's shortcake shop shut?
Is Sherry's shortcake shop shut?

*How many times can you say this
in ten seconds?*
   Soft smooth snake skin.

**How many slim, slimy snakes
   would slither silently to the sea,
If slim, slimy snakes
   could slither silently?**

**Smart, small snakes smell thick smoked steaks.
Smart, small snakes smell thick smoked steaks.
Smart, small snakes smell thick smoked steaks.**

Sharp sharkskin shoes.
Sharp sharkskin shoes.
Sharp sharkskin shoes.

Sixty-six sticky skeletons.
Sixty-six sticky skeletons.
Sixty-six sticky skeletons.

*How many times can you say this
in ten seconds?*
Sad skunk.

**Sloppy skiers slide on
slick ski slopes.**

How many times can you say
this in ten seconds?

Such a shapeless sash!

Scams, stings, and skulduggery.
Scams, stings, and skulduggery.
Scams, stings, and skulduggery.

Mr. Spink thinks the Sphinx stinks.
Mr. Spink thinks the Sphinx stinks.
Mr. Spink thinks the Sphinx stinks.

Thick ticks think thin ticks are sick.
Thick ticks think thin ticks are sick.
Thick ticks think thin ticks are sick.

How many times can you say this in ten seconds?
Theo saw three sly thrushes.

Tea for the thin twin tinsmith!
Tea for the thin twin tinsmith!
Tea for the thin twin tinsmith!

There goes one tough top cop.
There goes one tough top cop.
There goes one tough top cop.

Unsung songs.
Unsung songs.
Unsung songs.

Vicious visitors vexed the village.
Vicious visitors vexed the village.
Vicious visitors vexed the village.

The wretched witch watched a walrus
   washing.
Did the wretched witch watch a walrus
   washing?
If the wretched witch watched a walrus
   washing,
Where's the washing walrus the
   wretched witch watched?

If two witches watched
   two watches,
Which witch would
   watch which
   watch?

How many times can you say this in ten seconds?

Which wristwatch is a Swiss wristwatch?

**I wish I hadn't washed this wristwatch.
I washed all the wheels and the works.
Since this wristwatch got all washed,
Oh, how it jumps and jerks!**

**Wyatt wondered why the worn wires weren't
wrapped right.
Wyatt wondered why the worn wires weren't
wrapped right.
Wyatt wondered why the worn wires weren't
wrapped right.**

Wild wrens wing westward.
Wild wrens wing westward.
Wild wrens wing westward.

How many times can you say this in ten seconds?

One really wet red whale.

Wee Willie Winkie risks three wishes.
Wee Willie Winkie risks three wishes.
Wee Willie Winkie risks three wishes.

Weary railroad workers.
Weary railroad workers.
Weary railroad workers.

Agnes's X's are excellent.
Agnes's X's are excellent.
Agnes's X's are excellent.

Yesterday Yuri yelled at Euwell.
Usually, Euwell yells at Yuri.

The ex-egg-examiner.
The ex-egg-examiner.
The ex-egg-examiner.

This is Suzie's sister's zither.
This is Suzie's sister's zither.
This is Suzie's sister's zither.

Zithers slither slowly south.
Zithers slither slowly south.
Zithers slither slowly south.

*How many times can you say this
in ten seconds?*
Zack's backpack.

INDEX